# What Are YOU Waiting For?

*11 Action Steps To Giving Yourself the
Green Light in Life!*

**Eugene Bell Jr.**

Alex,

Don't wait, live your dreams now!

Eugene Bell

**What Are YOU Waiting For?**
*11 Action Steps to Giving Yourself the Green Light in Life!*

Published by: Bell Investment Group, LLC. a Pennsylvania Corporation

Printed in the United States of America

First Printing March of 2011

Library of Congress

2011902005

ISBN 978-0-9834386-0-1

Cover Design: Shaun Baron
Author's Photograph: Cecil E. Rudd

# Acknowledgements

It would require another book to include all the names of people who have or continue to directly or indirectly inspire me. It seems fitting for me to dedicate "What Are YOU Waiting For?", my first book, to two people who have always given me the green light in life:

Allison Walker, my mother!

Your unconditional love and belief in me have always provided a source of strength for me. Even at times when my own belief in self may have not been as strong, I knew I could lean on yours. You are the epitome of Mother and Friend and for that I am forever grateful!

Msgr. Wilfred Pashley, my father-figure!

You have shown me that biology has no bearing on being a Father. In my life you have certainly been teacher, protector, provider, and friend. Most importantly...You have been there since the beginning! I want you to know I recognize that and will never take it for granted.

"What you leave to someone isn't as important as what you leave in someone." Although it's not designed for a child to repay parents directly, I strive to pay it forward through mentoring young people, inspiring others, and successfully leading a family of my own.

Lastly, thank you to everyone who has ever given me an encouraging word, for that gave me the green light as well!

**What Are YOU Waiting For?** Start Reading ;)

# Table of Contents

# Introduction

"What Are YOU Waiting For?" is the culmination of ideas I've gathered and applied over the last 10 years. I joined a network marketing company which heavily promoted the importance of personal development and I bought in completely. And so my journey of personal development began.

Like many of you, I took the "traditional" educational route. Upon completing high school I continued on to graduate with a business degree from a respected university. Although I received a great education, I felt there was so much more I was missing. Mathematics, science, history, etc. are absolutely important in our development and I started to learn that there are other critical characteristics necessary to live a successful life. I heard one of my favorite mentors, Mr. Jim Rohn, once say, "Formal education will earn you a living, while self education can earn you a fortune." I believe the fortune to which he is referring isn't just about the financial aspect of life. There are the emotional, spiritual, physical, and relational fortunes included as well to create a successful life.

Having great success in one area while partially or completely neglecting the others does not constitute a successful life.

In "What Are YOU Waiting For?" I've included 11 steps you can use to create the successful life you know you deserve. Some steps require you to take physical action while others encourage a mental shift. One can never overstate the importance of mindset in accomplishing desired goals. Mindset will shape your philosophy, which goes to dictate your action, which will ultimately determine your result. What do time-honored sayings such as, "your attitude determines your altitude," "they can because they think they can," "mind-sight determines eye sight," and "winners have simply formed the habit of doing things losers don't like to do" all have in common? They all address the inner workings of the 6 inches between your ears before asking you to take physical action.

If you will commit to these 11 steps, I'm certain you will experience great positive change in many aspects of your life. I'm not sure where this book finds you. For some, you may possess three of the four numbers in your success combination and an idea here will serve as the catalyst to assist you in discovering the last piece. To you I say, congratulations in advance! For others, your success journey is just beginning and I'm excited to share in your experience. And to you as well I say, congratulations in advance! I am humbled and honored by the opportunity to participate in your development.

My suggestion is that you read this book twice within the first 30 days. The first time, just read through and absorb the information. Then on your second reading be sure to have a pen or pencil in hand to take notes and write ideas as they avail themselves to you. Underline, circle, and do whatever else you feel necessary to increase your ability to gain insight from *What Are YOU Waiting For?* I remember, as I was first getting into personal development, never wanting to mark up my books. Fortunately, I quickly learned what I was missing. Now when I reread a book, an idea I've previously highlighted stands out and I can determine if I've applied the concept or if it's an idea I need to revisit.

In our society we understand the red traffic signal to mean stop, yellow to mean caution or slow down (although many take it as a sign to go faster ☺), and green signifying GO! Allow this book to serve as the driver in the car behind you lightly blowing the horn because you have the green light!

**GO!**

# 1. Do It N.O.W. {it's *Not Over* until you *Win*}

## "Take just one more step..." -Marathon Runner

## Conquer Procrastination

Procrastination. The word sounds like a disease and to many its more debilitating than anything an M.D. could diagnose. And the challenge is, more likely than not, if you were to get a physical your Dr. wouldn't say, "oh I know the root of your problem, you've got procrastination!" Although it won't show up on any physical, we only need to look at our results and the symptoms of procrastination become glaringly apparent. I once read that procrastination is the bad habit of putting off until the day after tomorrow what should have been done the day before yesterday. This captures the essence of procrastination perfectly and I know you can relate. We've all had something we know we should have started or completed by "now " and of course "now" may have passed for you but I'm sure you get the point. In fact, this very book has been in me for years and since I allowed procrastination to stop by, pull up a chair, and have a drink I'm just getting it to you and for that I apologize! If any of this resonates with your spirit, continue reading. If not, skip this chapter because you're not of this planet! But seriously, we all know the grip of procrastination is strong and the key is to move with speed and boldness immediately before it can rear its ugly head. I was taught to whisper, "do it now, do it now, do it now" as an affirmation all day and specifically when I feel myself getting closer to saying, "oh I'll do it tomorrow" or "I'll do it later." Of course we know later and tomorrow never come so our rationaLIEzation is futile. When asked about his fears, Denzel Washington had this to say, " I'd be more frightened by not using whatever abilities I'd been given. I'd be more frightened by procrastination and laziness." I think once we take self-inventory we can uncover the root of our procrastination which, I'm sure, for many people is some fear. In my opinion, when you strip away all the layers there are only 3 main fears namely, the fear of failure, the fear of success, and the fear of death. Interesting tidbit: Statistically the fear of public speaking ranks above the fear of death. But of course the fear of public speaking is really the fear of looking/sounding stupid/unintelligent which is ultimately, the fear of failure. Throughout this book we need to take personal inventory to uncover the source of our procrastination.

2

# Personal Inventory Procrastination Test

1. Top 2-3 actions I know I must take to catapult me to the next level (ex. Gym membership, sales call, certain conversation I've avoided, cleaning, etc.)

2. How has not doing negatively impacted my life? (haven't gotten that raise, lack of time with family, missed opportunities, stress on my shoulders, etc.)

3. In not doing, there must be a belief in my subconscious about the outcome. What's the worst that could happen? (someone tells me 'no', I cause controversy, etc.)

4. Since the majority of us are not psychic we have no way of knowing that the outcomes we wrote in question 3 will come to fruition which means at any given moment, since we are in creation mode, it is our choice to create in our minds the vision of what we'd like to see or allow the fear of a negative outcome to fester. Having said that, let's expect that all will go our way, that Life will grant us what we demand. What's the outcome if you take the actions described in question#1 and it goes exactly as you want it to go? (promotion, start your own successful business, a more amazing relationship with a loved one)

As I alluded to in question 4, the place in which we currently stand is somewhat of a fork in the road. Visualize with me for a minute. You have this thing you know you must do, you want to do, you should do. The road to the left leads to Procrastination Station and the road right leads to Dreams Pkwy. All your life you've only

3

looked left and allowed the voice of procrastination to convince you there is no other way, that all your fears will be realized if you take action. You simply need only turn your head right and you will see clearly down Dreams Pkwy. Long ago I heard, "where focus goes, energy flows." So just the act of focusing on accomplishing your goals puts you in the power position of attracting that which you seek. Back to the fork in the road. You look right and you see all the outcomes you desire. It's a sunny well lit path, think your perfect definition of a spring day. Only you can determine what lives down that road for you and your family. There is nothing to stop you from mentally walking down that path. It is your choice to focus on the outcomes you want or to allow procrastination to keep you in a choke hold. So often this is the major challenge for us all and this is what I so passionately want to help you conquer.

## Aiming for 2<sup>nd</sup> Best Won't Win You the Presidency

Time and time again I've witnessed the reality of this choice in my own life. Allow me to share a personal example with you of an event in my life where initially I hesitated because of fear. I looked left instead of right. Fortunately I had someone in my life inspire

4

me to turn my head. Many years ago as I moved from 7<sup>th</sup> to 8<sup>th</sup> grade our school had student council elections. Immediately I wanted to be President but looked left and had the thought of running and loosing. Also I thought, "I'm an inner-city black kid going to a predominantly white school in a rich neighborhood and there is no way I will get voted in." So I decided to run for Vice-President. As I mentioned, I had someone to help direct my vision right. My mom asked why I wasn't running for President and I don't remember if I ever gave her my real answer or any answer for that matter because no answer would have sufficed. I remember her saying, "never aim for second, never short change yourself." She went on further to say, you can win, let's go for President! Can't say no to mom right? My campaign management team consisted of my mom and Msgr. Wilfred Pashley, a Catholic priest who has been a father figure in my life since the beginning. With them having my back there was no way I could go wrong and at the end of the campaign we arose victorious! That was the start of my understanding of the importance of focusing on what you want and taking immediate action toward that outcome rather than focusing on what you don't want.

You may have heard F.E.A.R. is nothing but False Evidence Appearing Real. Most often it's a figment of our imagination, some mental construct we've allowed to hinder us from achieving goals we know are our destiny. Too many of us are standing at the edge not realizing we're wearing wings and once we jump, instinct will take over and we will spread our wings to soar with the eagles. Do It N.O.W.!

Now is all we have! One of my favorite sayings is Yesterday is History and Tomorrow is a Mystery, Today aka NOW is all we have. Treat the present as the gift it is and move immediately toward your goal. In talking about the value of today, now, this moment, acclaimed author Og Mandino, in The Greatest Secret in the World, instructs us to live this day as if it is our last. He proceeds with:

"I will waste not a moment mourning yesterday's misfortunes, yesterday's defeats, yesterday's aches of the heart, for why should I throw good after bad.......And what then shall I do? Forgetting yesterday neither will I think of tomorrow. Why should I throw *now* after *maybe*? Can tomorrow's sand flow through the glass before today's? Will the sun rise twice this morning? Can I perform tomorrow's deeds while standing in today's path? Can I place tomorrow's gold in today's purse? Should I torment myself with problems that may never come to pass? No! Tomorrow lies buried with yesterday, and I will think of it no more." Do it N.O.W.!

Time is one currency, once spent, we can never recover. Do it N.O.W.!

The only person stopping you is you! Do it N.O.W.!

"Procrastination is the assassination of your final destination!" Do it N.O.W.!

Guard your mind like a ferocious beast against the thief of time aka fear. Do it N.O.W.!

## Successful v. Unsuccessful

What separates the successful from the unsuccessful so many times is that the successful simply do it. They take action, they aren't necessarily smarter than others; they simply just do it. The time to act is when the emotion is strong. Because if you don't, here's what happens - it's called the law of diminishing intent. We intend to act when the idea hits us, when the emotion is high, but if we wait around and we don't translate that into action fairly soon, the intention starts to diminish, and a month from now it's cold and a year from now it can't be found. So set up the discipline when the idea is strong, clear and powerful - that's the time to work the plan. Here's what is key: all disciplines affect each other; everything affects everything. That's why the smallest action is important --

7

because the value and benefits that you receive from that one little action will inspire you to do the next one and the next one... Step out and take action today on your plan because if the plan is good, then the results can be amazing.

**Eric Rosen**
**Internet Marketing Specialist**
http://OnlineLocalEdgeMarketing.com/

## It's Not Over Until YOU Win!

A part of the Do It N.O.W. philosophy is the understanding that it's Not Over until I Win. I encourage you to adopt this for yourself and I know one of you reading this is saying, "But you can't always win." I disagree! If the score says you lost and you learned something in the process which can assist you in the future, you have, in actuality, won! It's all in your attitude! I'm headed into my 5th year of coaching youth basketball and during my 3rd year, regarding talent, arguably we had the best team in the league. We were favored to get to the championship if not win it all. We ran a smothering full court 3-2 press defense which, due to the athleticism and tenacity of our starting five, began to conjure fear in the opponents before we stepped on the court. Our team started the season 8-0 and then I was blindsided by injuries and other challenges within our team for which I had not prepared us. As a result we started losing because I had not properly prepared our bench on whom we now had to rely. Nevertheless in spite of the setbacks our players fought hard and we ended up making it into the final four that season. Some may say, see there, you lost. Once again, I disagree! I looked back at the season to find the lessons and this is where I realized I focused too much on the starting five and not enough on developing our whole team to reach their full potential. Maybe if teams everywhere, in the athletic arena, business community, etc., would focus on developing the whole team it wouldn't be so easy for a setback to knock them off course. How many times have you seen a team's game plan rocked because the franchise player was lost due to injury or misconduct? I think this is why Hall of Fame coaches like John Wooden, former coach of the UCLA Bruins, are so successful. He focused on developing and inspiring every player to reach their full potential. As I sat looking back at the season, when this realization availed itself to me I could only smile. No need to beat myself up, no need to be angry with anyone. We had a great run, lots of fun, and I learned not just a coaching lesson but a life lesson which was, in the great word of Mastercard, ...Priceless!

**So it's not over until YOU win!**

## 2. Talk About It and Be About It

**"For 1500 years, the Earth was the center of the Solar System simply because Claudius Ptolemy said so. A week before Kittyhawk a New York science editor proved that heavier-than-air-flight was impossible. Experts at first said James Joyce couldn't write, Picasso couldn't paint, and Elvis couldn't sing. What do they say about you?" –Dare To Be Different**

### Speak It Into Existence

Often times you  may have said or heard someone else say, "don't talk about it, be about it." Understanding the basic message one would attempt to convey with that statement, don't JUST talk about it, get it done, I have a bit of a different take on it.  I say talk about it AND be about it!  The talking about it can aide in the being about it.  That's what positive affirmations are all about, speaking dreams into existence.  I've seen this work countless times in my life, many times when others didn't believe it could be done.  I remember a time when I was younger there was a beautiful car I just had to have.  Day in and day out for 2 years I talked about getting this car and of course many around me didn't believe it was going to happen.  I never gave up on it, I believed it already belonged to me and the dealership was just storing it for me. December of that year just before Christmas break for college I was telling people at school that I was coming back with this car I'd been talking about for the previous two years and of course I was met with disbelief. Some with just a nonchalant attitude and others with a downright "no you're not!" That January it was so sweet to pull up on campus with a beautiful Acura Legend! Now hind sight is 20/20 and 1. I was blessed to have a mother who believed in my belief of owning that vehicle and 2. Financially at the time it probably wasn't the best move so don't mistake my message here for me saying you need to go out and put yourself deep in debt for a liability. It sure felt good though especially when the naysayers then started to say, "Well you said you were going to get it!" As if they believed me all the time. I'm a firm believer in the Law of Attraction and there is something magical in the Talking About something while being about it. Add passion, belief, and conviction to your Talk and the universe begins to move in your favor. The right people show up in your life or some seemingly chance opportunity avails itself to you. You have to have the audacity to believe that whatever you desire is already yours. If it's that luxury automobile, beautiful home, or multimillion dollar investment portfolio. It's already yours. Own it! Money is an easy by-product to measure, so let's say you have a goal of earning $150K, $500K, or $1M per year. Once you hit that target how will you walk, how will you talk? I say begin to walk and talk it now. Put the Law of Attraction to work for you.

## How Much Are You Worth?

**True story:** A friend of mine has been talking about wanting to start her own travel business for as long as I can remember and in reality she was the catalyst for the title of this book. She had just started working in the call center of a well known rail company here in the U.S. The training period was 4 months, 2 months in the classroom and 2 months on the call center floor. At the end of the training period they were given a "graduation" reception to celebrate their qualification. She produced the most revenue of her class for the 2 months on the call center floor. $131,000 to be exact during the 2 months! Now this is a job she knew didn't pay commission so there was no gripe there. Here is where the rub comes in. She was given a certificate in recognition of her achievement...based on what happened next, I feel this is where it should have been left. Attached to the certificate was a Wawa gift card. Wawa, if you don't know, is a convenience store chain. There was not an amount listed on the gift card and one would assume the card would have $20 or maybe even $25 on it. She went to Wawa, purchased a gallon of milk for $3.79 after taxes. Are you ready for this? Her receipt said the remaining card balance was $1.21. Do the math... that was a $5.00 gift card. Ouch! This woman generated $131,000+ of revenue during the previous 2 months and in gratitude she was given a certificate and a $5.00 gift card. Does anyone see anything wrong with this picture? After hearing this, I immediately asked her What Are YOU Waiting For? I knew that was to be the title of this book. I said to her, "you obviously know your stuff, you've been in the travel business for years and if there is a more clear indicator out there that you're never going to get paid your worth working at that company, I've never seen it." I couldn't believe it, they were paying her $12.80/hr with no commission. She generated $131,000 within 2 months and was given a $5.00 gift card. So she has half my equation down, she's doing the talking about it and now she needs to do the being about it. She talks about wanting it. She knows the business. She obviously can sell. She only needs to be about it and take action on her desire to create a world class travel business. 1. You'll be able to dictate your worth to the marketplace rather than having a company say you're worth $12.80/hr to us. 2. You won't have to experience the embarrassment of a company trading your $131,000 of production for a $5.00 convenient store gift card.

Don't misunderstand me here as saying everyone should walk off of their jobs today. No! Jobs serve a purpose and some love what they do and are able to live the life they desire. There is the other majority out there who feel deep in their gut, "this isn't it for me, I'm worth more, I'm meant to contribute and achieve more thereby getting more from the marketplace."

## Guard Your Dreams

Life is to be lived to the fullest and if there is anything getting in the way of you living your passion it's time to talk about it and be about the business of designing your desired lifestyle. I can hear some of you saying, "well you can't really talk about your dreams with everyone." I completely agree. There are a variety of reasons why one shouldn't discuss their dreams and aspirations with everyone, we will cover only one here…negativity! As the old saying goes, some folks are so negative that if they walked into a dark room they'd develop. I recognize this and you should as well. When you are at the beginning stages of accomplishing your dreams, often times before you even set out, there are folks who will go all out in the sales pitch on why you shouldn't go after "that" dream. Let's discuss two reasons for this. 1. They may have attempted living their dreams in the past and didn't have your stick-to-it-tiveness so they met with failure, and it was only real failure because they got knocked down and decided not to get back up. 2. They believe if you're as wildly successful as you know you will be, they have a deep, albeit unconscious, fear of losing you to the world. Taking a deeper look at reason one, on the surface we can understand why a loved one may feel a need to "protect" you from that experience. He or she may say, "I've tried that and it doesn't work" or "no one ever makes money that way" or "you have a good job so why risk it, just be happy with what you have." And to them this sounds like wise advice but in reality what they are doing, especially if you allow this conversation to dissuade you, is stealing your dreams. Your mom, dad, sister, brother, aunt, uncle, husband, or wife may have tried "that" network marketing business before, may have attempted to write the book, or even taken a shot at self employment. They failed, were rejected, or just didn't have the lasting success they expected and wrongly assume you'll meet with the same fate. And you know what they say when a person assumes! Once a person has been knocked down, the longer they stay down, the more challenging it is to get up. This is why when a person is learning to ride a horse and they fall, they are instructed to immediately hop back on and not allow the fear to build. The same goes for our dreams. When life delivers a devastating blow in your pursuit of your dreams, and make no mistake life will hit hard at a time when you least expect it and from an angle which was just outside of your peripheral, it is imperative that you jump immediately back on that "horse" and keep it moving. At this point the power of talking and being about it are extremely pertinent. The positive affirmations and the encouraging conversations, the talking about it, with others can aide in a speedy recovery as you jump right back in the ring and go for another round, the being about it. Ding...Ding! I believe we can learn something from all sources so this doesn't mean turn a deaf ear to anyone who says they've tried something in the past. It simply means to keep all we hear in proper context, if we gather useful information, apply it, otherwise discard it. We all learn from our own experiences and the experiences of others. Everything is about taking action, correcting that action, and taking more action. You take a step with your right foot to correct the step you took with your left foot as you navigate your way to your destination. I'm reminded of something I once heard Jim Rohn, world renowned business leader, say "if you read that book it says eat this and you'll live a long life and this book over here says if you do what that first book says you'll die young." He then goes onto say, "read both books and make up your own mind." So both a success and a failure can teach us a lesson. The key is to keep everything in context.

## Avoid the Crabs

Let's glance at the reason 2. We all have a comfort zone within which we inhabit. This goes for foods we're willing to try, adventures we're willing to take, as well as people we keep close to us. You may be surrounded by small minded people, or as we like to say, people with the crabs in the barrel mentality. Certainly you've seen crabs in the containers waiting to be sold, as one makes a move to get out the others grab hold to bring it right back down to the level of every other crab. Unfortunately there are people like this in our lives. Some do it consciously because they don't want to see you succeed and others do it subconsciously because your current station is within their comfort zone. If you experience success, they fear you will leave them or your success will further illuminate their perceived lack. I guess it's the old misery loves company philosophy. You really have to watch out for these folks, unfortunately at times these can be some of the closest people to you. They can sabotage your efforts with subtlety and you will look up one day and wonder why you've either never tried or how you ended up so off course. What they fail to realize is that a sinking ship never sends an S.O.S. to another sinking ship so if they contribute to your success it can assist you in accomplishing your goals faster which could put you in a much better position to lend a helping hand to assist them in accomplishing their goals.

## When 1 + 1 = 3 or More

Another benefit of talking to the right people is the benefit of the Master Mind. When 2 people come together for the purpose of sharing good ideas and accomplishing goals a third more powerful mind is created. You may frame something in a manner which makes it more clear for me and with this deeper understanding or awareness I'm better equipped to accomplish the goal at hand. A few months ago I was having a conversation with a friend, Mike Morrow, founder of Philadelphia Status. We were informally just throwing ideas around and brainstorming about his business and a project on which I was working. He made a statement which really helped me determine a direction in which to move with my project. Mike asked if I had ever heard of the Commander's Intent. I said no and he went on to explain "the Commander's Intent is a military term which by definition is a concise expression of the purpose of the operation and the desired end state that serves as the initial reason for the planning process." Basically, what is your desired outcome? He continued, "in looking at your business, with every decision you must ask yourself, does this move you toward your Commander's Intent or take you away?" So first you have to define that desired outcome, or Commander's Intent, and then use that as the filter through which you take all ideas related to the project. This forces you to not only see what's happening at ground level

20

but also to take a global view. As I said, hindsight is 20/20 and looking back it makes so much sense and having that conversation with Mike really helped me to shift my thinking. If we weren't talking about it, the being about it would have remained more challenging.

# 3. Commit to Personal Development

**"The most important question to ask on the job is not "What am I getting?" The most important question to ask is "What am I becoming?"**
**—Jim Rohn, America's Foremost Business Philosopher**

## Sharpen Your Ax

Over the last few years, Personal Development has become a great passion of mine. Ben Franklin said, "if I have 4 hours to chop down a tree, I'd spend 3 hours sharpening my ax." As we interpret that statement, we understand the ax to be him and the tree whatever endeavor upon which he has embarked. Stated another way, he'd spend more time sharpening himself and his skills than he would on the actual task at hand. Sometimes you just hear something that resonates with your spirit immediately and this was one such example. Personal development is exactly that, personal. So I would not presume to tell you exactly what you need, only you know your challenge areas or the areas that if you improve 1% everyday it would make a huge difference. I CAN tell you that you have the ability to continuously improve. Where you are today physically, mentally, emotionally, financially, and/or spiritually has nothing to do with where you can be tomorrow.

## 21-Day Personal Development Challenge

1. **Cut off the TV and don't read the newspaper**: FIFO and LIFO are inventory terms meaning First In First Out and Last In Last Out respectively. Regarding matters of the mind, it can be said another way, NINO and PIPO, Negative In, Negative Out and Positive In, Positive Out. What you put in is the only thing that can come out. Only in a magician's world can you stuff a hat with scarves and pull out a rabbit. If you fill your life with negative thoughts and negative people, you will have a negative outlook and experience. I rarely watch the news and when I do I'm looking for the weather and major sports scores of a favorite team. Other than that, overall it's a depressing show. The majority of the news is about some violence somewhere in the world and then they give a little 2 minute blurb on a positive event happening in the community. Test: Watch the news and write the headline from each

story. Then list how many of the items discussed directly impact your life. I'd be willing to bet not many. The problem with filling our heads with so much nothingness is there is no middle ground, if something isn't contributing to you it's taking away from you. It's either moving you toward or away from your goals. I challenge you to turn off the TV and not read the newspaper for 21 days. Of course if there is information you need to assist you in your job or business, acquire it but even with that, since we're living in the digital age, I'd imagine you can conduct a quick search online and find the specific information needed.

2. **Avoid Gossip**: This means not only are you committed to not gossiping but you also steer clear of gossipers. It's rare that gossip is positive. Usually people are somewhere in private pointing out the negatives about another person. Interesting thing about gossip, it takes from you as much if not more than it takes from the person being gossiped about. I say this because in order for you to get involved in gossip garbage gab you have to sink lower to pull someone

else down. Plus gossip never resolves any issues because we're not actually telling the person with whom we have the issue. It begins to grow and fester and by the time we are ready to confront the person it's done from a position of anger and frustration rather than one of empowerment and effective communication. Some of us have been doing it so much and for so long that gossiping has become a way of life.

3. **Read 10 pages and listen to 10 minutes of uplifting and encouraging material daily:** Books such as Think and Grow Rich by Napoleon Hill, The Success Principles by Jack Canfield, 21 Irrefutable Laws of Leadership by John C. Maxwell, Og Mandino's Trilogy of The Greatest Salesman in the World, The Greatest Secret in the World, and The Greatest Miracle in the World, and of course What Are YOU Waiting For?, the book you're reading, are just a few I'd recommend. Quality audio sets such as Law of Attraction by Esther and Jerry Hicks, Choosing Your Future by Les Brown, and The Art of Exceptional Living by

Jim Rohn are great tools to help you turn your vehicle into D.T.U., Drive Time University.

4.  **Execute:** I'm sure you've heard knowledge is power, well there is a word missing from that statement. The more accurate statement says APPLIED knowledge is power, emphasis on applied. Without application, you having the knowledge is worth as much as not having it. You KNOW you're supposed to eat a healthy diet and exercise regularly but if you don't do what you know where are you? So we must be sure to not only gain the knowledge but also, as the iconic Nike slogan instructs us, Just Do It!

I've always been somewhat of a glass-half-full type of guy and as I became more and more passionate about personal development it was easier and easier to maintain a positive attitude. And maintaining that positive attitude enables you to navigate the 4 Stages of Consciousness, a lesson I've learned along the way from many trainers so I wouldn't know exactly who gets the credit. Suffice it to say, I didn't create it but I know it to be true from personal experience so I will share it with you on the next page.

Personal development simply makes life easier because as you become better, you produce better. The 4 Stages of Consciousness are present in everything we've learned in life from walking to riding a bike to driving a car and much more. Let's take a look:

## 4 Stages of Consciousness

1. **Unconsciously Incompetent:** You don't know what you don't know. Before you've made any attempt to learn a new skill there really is no way of knowing all of what you'll need to know to become proficient. Arrogance often lives here so it's important to remain open and understand you'll need to learn a new skill set. I love to drive and when I first was ready to learn I thought I knew enough just by watching others. I quickly found out there was so much I didn't know about the feel of various automobiles, handling different driving conditions, recognizing certain signs, etc. Now we move to..

2. **Consciously Incompetent:** Now you KNOW you don't know. This is a good place to be because this is usually where humility sets in and an openness occurs. In our

driving example, I realized in order to become a better driver there were skills I needed to learn. It drove me, pun intended, to seek out answers from those who had been driving far longer than I had. After staying here for awhile we now transition to...

3.  **Consciously Competent:** Confidence begins to build here as you realize you know it, you just have to concentrate more intently on the task at hand. I remember moving into this stage as I was learning to drive. I would drive around in silence, no radio, if there were folks in the car with me, they needed to keep quiet so I could focus on the road, gauges, and other vehicles. The old saying, "practice makes improvement," rings true here. The more you practice proper technique the better and more confident you become. Confidence feeds into competence which then feeds right back into confidence and so the cycle continues as you move to...

4.  **Unconsciously Competent:** You KNOW that you know and its AUTOMATIC. As a toddler, walking was a huge

challenge and of course you tried and fell and tried and fell and tried and....walked. Before long you were running. Now, when was the last time you concentrated on walking? Its unconscious now, its automatic. You've established the habit pattern which allows you to put walking on autopilot which frees you up to walk, text, and chew gum at the same time. Completing our driving example, now I can simultaneously drive, listen to the radio, have a conversation with a passenger, and follow directions from the GPS system. Repetition is the mother of all learning. This is the reason professional athletes spend hours in the gym continuously repeating the same series of shots or moves. They are creating the habit patterns which allow for automatic action so in that split second when the game is on the line they are unconsciously competent. For the sports lovers out there, you'll have heard this before, especially in basketball when a player seems to be making any and everything she throws at the basket. You'll hear the commentator or maybe you have said it, "she's unconscious!"

As I mentioned, personal development assists us in creating and maintaining the automatic positive attitude which then enables us to navigate the 4 Stages of Consciousness more effectively and efficiently. This is everywhere, in doing, thinking, and being, we pass through the 4 Stages of Consciousness.

## Associations

Birds of a feather flock together...If you were raised anything like me this is a saying you heard often. Parents recognize the importance of monitoring who their children call friends. We become like those with whom we most associate. There are two sides to this phenomenon. You must get around a group of people that have what you want and are headed where you're headed. You also must become worthy to be a part of this group because they too recognize the importance of guarding their associations. They realize you will have an effect on who they become as well.

## Nothing Much v. Everything!

As I mentioned on the previous page: repetition is the mother of all learning. Sound familiar? Do you remember your beginning multiplication table lessons? What's 2 x 2, or 12 x 12? Of course you know the answers are 4 and 144 respectively. Our teachers and parents had us repeat them so often, the first 12 are ingrained deeply in us. Quickly what's 13 x 14? Sure some may know it immediately but if you're anything like me, that's one you'll need to work out rather than just "knowing" it since that wasn't on the memorization list. How about the concept of positive affirmations? The idea of speaking positively to ourselves. Affirmations don't have to be in the form of some elaborate speech. One of the simplest I know of...Nike's Just Do It! Other examples: "I can do it" or "Everyday in every way I'm getting better and better" or "I'm someone special." Affirmations come, unfortunately, in the negative as well. You ever find yourself saying something like, "It'll be just my luck...?" Usually when we utter that phrase we end it with something negative. We're saying it's just my luck that something bad is going to happen or things aren't going my way, correct? I'm a firm believer with every fiber of my being that all is supposed to work out in my favor. I know great things are supposed to happen to me. It's my birthright! Yours as well! Earlier in life I questioned, do things work out for me because I believe they're supposed to or do I believe they're supposed to because they work out for me? I'd imagine its some combination of both with a greater responsibility for the outcome stemming out of my positive belief.

We've created many habits in our lives, many we've forgotten about long ago, ie. which pant leg you put on first or which side of your mouth gets brushed first or the way you arrange your clothes, etc. And of course we can continue that list for pages. All of what I just mentioned are arguably trivial habits at best. Fact is though, they are habits nonetheless which is not necessarily a bad thing. Habits allow us to go on auto pilot, they enable us to redistribute our thinking resources to items we feel require our active attention. According to Aristotle, "we are what we repeatedly do. Excellence then, is not an act, but a habit." Rob Gilbert goes on to say, "first we form habits, then they form us. Conquer your bad habits, or they will conquer you." Developing the habit of repeating positive affirmations throughout your day will positively change your world! That being said, lets discuss Nothing Much vs. Everything! We've established that the things we repeatedly say or do have a positive or negative effect on us. A few years back, as I was getting more into personal development, I began taking inventory on self. What are my habits, how does my self-talk sound? Changing some habits required major focus, others, not so much. I've never been a smoker but from what I'm told, that's a habit which presents a major challenge for folks, and we know that's a negative one. It serves the person no way and no how! An anonymous author suggested, "Bad habits are like a comfortable bed, easy to get into but hard to get out of." I'm sure you can relate! Getting back to habits I changed, I realized there was something I was saying multiple times a day which could only take me away from my goals. Perhaps you're like me on this one. And we say it many different ways, we'll look at a couple here. You and I are friends. When we see each other or speak, one of us asks, "What's up?" or "What's going on?" The most common response given by 99.9% of people I know? "Nothing Much!" Said another way, "Same soup, reheated." Think about that for a second. Someone asks you what's going on in your life and the common response is nothing much. Rephrased: There is nothing much going on in my life. Or there is nothing up in my life. Keep tabs on yourself today and track your responses.

After noticing my responses, I decided to make an immediate change. When people ask me what's up or what's going on, my response is, with enthusiasm and posture, **"EVERYTHING!"** Everything IS up in my life, everything is going on in my life! Why would I respond any other way? At first you'll feel very hokie and then as with any other habit, when done often enough, it feels normal. Now I couldn't imagine telling someone nothing is up in my life. At the very least you'll get a smile out of the person to whom you're speaking. How much is a smile worth? Priceless! You will begin to feel a power in you every time you respond, "Everything!" You can use that inner feeling to propel you throughout your day. Positively charge your self-talk and replace your bad habits with habits which serve you and watch the transition in your life! Answering with **"EVERYTHING!"** is a way to simultaneously accomplish both!

# 4. Focus on Future

**"Imagination is everything. It is the preview of life's coming attractions." –Albert Einstein**

## Time Machine

Where do you see yourself in 6 months, 1, 5, or 10yrs? Really take time to answer this question for yourself. Is what you're currently doing going to provide the type of life you'd like for you and your family? Will it provide the mental, spiritual, and emotional sustenance you require? If you are one of the very few people who can answer yes to either or both of those questions, congratulations! You would however, fall into the category of the exception and not the rule. The ability to answer yes to one or both questions is extremely rare. Are there aspects of your life where you'd like to see improvement? No matter who you are or what your circumstances may be, there is always another level to which we can aspire! This is why it's important to allow your future vision to pull you through your current challenges. This is not to say we shouldn't be grateful and content with our current station in life. There is a reason we are where we are so we should always express an attitude of gratitude and not allow complacency to set in. One night, we had an open forum conversation on the radio show I co-host, The Streets Are Talking'. These questions were asked, "Why is it that some people don't aspire to greatness, why don't they want more, and what can we do to inspire people?" In some communities and neighborhoods there is a collective lack of belief in their ability to have more. People fall into the, "this is how it was for my mom or my dad and this is how it will be for me," mode of thinking. I believe everyone has a desire to have and do more at the heart of their request however, they often believe massive success is for that other guy. There are two ways we can inspire people:

1. **Continue to Offer Empowering Information:** I love giving uplifting books and audio sets as gifts because I know these are tools which can assist a person in transitioning from their current spot on the success curve to their desired location. Also, like the ripple effect in a lake which appears to go on infinitely, I never know where the benefit of that gift stops. You give someone Think and Grow Rich by Napoleon Hill as a gift. They go on to

master the 13 characteristics of successful people and teach a group of young people lessons directly from that book. One young person gets inspired and decides to start a business which enables them to provide jobs and donate to charity. A beneficiary of the charity is so appreciative that she aspires to one day be in a position to give back as well, and the ripple continues. Sure the book, the initial stone to cause the ripple, may have only cost you a few bucks and a few minutes of your time shopping but what number can we put on the compounded value of all the ripples? Priceless!

2. **Be the Testimony:** I challenge you to be the success story that others can look up to. In network marketing we're always taught, facts tell and stories sell. Of course when you first join, you have no personal success of which to point so you get really good at telling the success stories of your leadership. This allows edification, simply speaking highly of someone else, to work in your favor. While telling the stories of others is vitally important, developing your

own success story is paramount because there does not exist a more powerful testimony for you and your group than your own. It's great to have the ability to point to another and highlight the success they've created for their family and imagine what it will mean for you to say, "this is where I was when I started and, as a result of following these success principles, look at me now!" And your purpose here isn't to brag or boast, you remain humble throughout the whole process, your purpose is to become the testimony for your neighborhood, organization, or community. Folks point to you and think, "If she can do it, I definitely can do it!" We realize it's not you, it's God's light shining through you as a beacon which provides direction for others to allow their light to shine.

## The Past: A Place of Reference not Residence

Yesterday doesn't dictate tomorrow unless you allow it to. The past has its place and purpose. Good memories inspire and motivate us to accomplish great memories. Memories of challenges are great teachers, we can either learn the pot is hot because we touched it or watched someone else touch it. Either way, we know if we touch it with bare hands again, ie. reliving the past, we will get burned. If you are attempting to drive from Philadelphia to Los Angeles while focusing 90% on your rearview mirrors I'd bet you wouldn't get off your street before you'd crash. It's impossible to successfully progress into the future with a rearward focus. I heard somewhere once, "if God wanted you to move backwards He would have reversed the direction of your feet and put eyes on the back of your head instead." We get so caught up in yesterday that we neglect today and certainly don't prepare for tomorrow. This is a vicious cycle. I remember having a debate about the importance of the past in relation to where you're headed. As far as knowing your cultural history and heritage, I believe the past can inspire and is very important. Other than that, the past is useful as a place of reference not a place of residence. Where you are and where you've been does not determine your final destination. If anything, it may only help to understand the length of time it will take to arrive. The best example I can give to illustrate this point is your GPS or navigation system in your vehicle. To arrive at a destination there are only two important coordinates, 1. Current Location and 2.

Desired Location. The GPS never asks where were you yesterday or 5 minutes ago. It only needs to know where you sit now and the address of your goal. With those two pieces of information it can successfully guide you from Philadelphia to Los Angeles. If you're like me, I'm sure over the years you've given driving directions to a friend. Maybe they called you midway to say they made a wrong turn and usually your first question to them is, especially if there are no street signs, "What do you see?" You never ask what they saw five minutes ago because that information serves no baring in your ability to provide directions. Your new financial planner won't ask for last year's net worth. He needs only to know your current net worth to effectively and efficiently guide you to your financial goals. Get the point?

## Back to the Future

Scripture says it's important to plant your seeds, cultivate and then harvest. The harvest takes place sometime in the future and we must allow the vision of that future harvest to push us into action today. Let's look at an iconic professional athlete such as Kobe Bryant. The seed of a successful NBA career was planted long ago.

Sure he's been gifted with certain talents and abilities but over the years he has put in thousands of hours of practice time, cultivating that seed. Now we see the harvest on game night as he proves to be unstoppable. Many kids I coach want to go straight from being in 6$^{th}$ or 7$^{th}$ grade to being Kobe since he makes it look so effortless at times. My job as coach is to help them see that Kobe has mastered the fundamentals through repetitive drills starting with something as basic as practicing the proper foot off which to jump for a right or left handed lay-up. In every industry there are those basic fundamentals you must master, so in focusing on the future we must not forget to plant the seed and cultivate in the present so we can reap the harvest in the future.

# 5. Enlist a Tour Guide

**"If you could find out what the most successful people did in any area and then you did the same thing over and over, you'd eventually get the same results they do." –Brian Tracy**

## A Few Days in the Call Center

I spent a brief period as an Amtrak Reservation Sales Agent taking calls for hours a day from travelers all across the country. The caller would tell me where they were leaving from and where they were headed. I'd plug that into the system and it would give back the train routes servicing those end points. I've been very fortunate to have traveled a lot in my life but there are still so many places I've never been and routes I've yet to take. Often the caller would ask certain specifics about a route or destination and I was unable to answer because I had never gone that way. I could speculate, I could ask someone else, or I would hope there was information in the system which would allow me to effectively answer their question. I began to notice that pertaining to places I've visited and routes I'd taken, I was so much more effective at selling the trip or accommodation. This is why it's better, on your life or business

45

journey, to Enlist a Tour Guide rather than a travel agent. Think about it, the tour guide walks the walk with you and the travel agent shows you nice pictures and sends you on your way. I've been to a lot of seminars and trainings where the presenter was giving us the "keys" or "success tips" to XYZ but the presenter had never used them. There is a reason why generally when a person gives their success testimonial it involves some tribulations. Have you ever heard a speaker get up before the crowd or write the book which says, "oh I just walked right in to the championship spot without any hard work, challenges, or effort!" Most likely not. A quote I like reads, "you can't have the TESTimony without the TEST. So give me the man or woman who has been there, done that and herein lies the power of enlisting a tour guide aka a Mentor.

## 4 Types of Knowledge

We learn 4 ways:

**Learned Knowledge:** Information we gather from reading the books and listening to the audio seminars and trainings. A person with a high learned knowledge IQ is said to have book smarts which is very important. *Learn by reading and listening.*

**Activity Knowledge:** This is where we learn by applying what we know, putting it into practice. We learn, do, obtain a deeper awareness and understanding, do again from an empowered position. Street smarts is the term used to describe a person with a high activity knowledge IQ. *Learn by doing.*

**Modeling Knowledge:** The quote, "It's ok to copycat as long as you copy the right cat" applies perfectly in this section. We watch others, gauge their results, and then choose to apply or disregard that lesson. When I first started presenting and training, I modeled other successful presenters and trainers until I established my own style which still is a blend of my own stuff and those I modeled. *Learn by watching.*

**Teaching Knowledge:** Once we've gotten proficient, we now have the opportunity to teach others. This gives us a deeper understanding because as Jim Rohn puts it, "when I strive to make it more clear for you, I make it more clear for myself." Have you ever tried teaching someone something you could do with your eyes closed and hands tied behind your back but then when you go to explain it you get tongue tied or feel as though you're not making yourself clear? You experience this strange phenomenon because there is a big difference between teaching and knowing for yourself. I've played basketball for as long as I can remember and it wasn't until I started coaching the youth that I really began to understand the game. *Learn by showing.*

Three of the four directly involve the Enlist a Tour Guide mentality. In learned knowledge, chances are we are reading the book or listening to the audio of someone who has walked the walk. With Modeling knowledge, I doubt you'd mimic a person who has not gotten the results you seek. And in Teaching Knowledge, you then become the Tour Guide.

## Signs You Have a Good Tour Guide

He or She:

1. has been to the place you're headed, using finances for this example, can a person earning $100K show you how to earn and maintain $1M?

2. understands the journey is yours and won't attempt to do it all for you but will assist you in navigating around pitfalls

3. is unselfish and willing to give you access to every success tool in their arsenal

4. isn't afraid to offer constructive criticism and understands the power of recognition and positive reinforcement

5. believes in you and your ability to make the journey

6. has successfully guided others

As I said, your Tour Guide isn't there to do it all for you so you must:

1. **Know** where you'd like to arrive, set goals, and create a plan

2. **Possess** a burning desire to succeed

3. **Remain** open to constructive criticism

4. **Believe** and know within yourself that you are able to successfully accomplish the goal

5. **Commit** to Tony Robbins' C.A.N.I.™, Constant and Never-ending Improvement

Back in the day, the family doctor was just that, the family's doctor. They treated the children as well as the adults and they treated the whole body. Now the children see the pediatrician, if you have a back problem you see the chiropractor, for heart problems the cardiologist, etc. We live in a world of specialization so it makes sense to have multiple tour guides for the various areas of our being. You might have a personal trainer, spiritual and/or religious guide, nutritionist, business coach, and whatever other type of guide you can imagine. I have a personal trainer, a saxophone instructor, multiple life coaches, an accountant, to name a few of the many Tour Guides in my life. All of these folks specialize and have all been or are where I'm headed in their respective fields. Enlist your Tour Guide!

# 6. Balance Work and Rest

"By setting limits for yourself and making the most of the resources you already have, you'll finally be able to work less, work smarter, and focus on living the life that you deserve."
—Leo Babauta, author of The Power of Less

## Bust a Gut

Have fun! Don't be so serious in life! Smile, laugh, dance! Let loose! Sometimes we get so caught up in the business of life that we forget to allow our inner child to run free. Have you ever met the man or woman who, on their death bed, requested more time to work? Nope! On a person's last day the wish usually is about having more time with family and friends, more time to walk the beaches of the world, see the sights, try the exotic cuisines, give more to the under-privileged, and the list is as varied as the number of people walking the planet. Everything in our universe is about balance. In accounting the right side must equal the left side of the equation. When your body temperature elevates, sweating is its mechanism to bring you back into balance. Your equilibrium is what enables you to walk upright without falling over. Balance. If we rest too much, we lack productivity. If we work too much, we rob the mind, body, and spirit of the necessary time to recover and grow.

## Unplug to Recharge

The promise of the digital age was for us to have the ability to be more productive in less time and we've gone overboard with our usage of the tools at our disposal. As a result we are plugged in 24hrs a day. I've sold cell phones for a number of different carriers throughout the years and I remember we used to tell customers it was important to power cycle, turn off, their phones at some point during the day or night. This gave the device an opportunity to reset and update. As humans we need to power cycle at times, just turn ourselves off. I know it's a challenge, I'm very connected to my mobile phone which, of course, now isn't just a mobile phone, it's a smart phone. I can check emails, send text messages, read and post on Facebook, Twitter, Google search, etc. all from the palm of my hand. Now it's necessary to have an Ipod and an Ipad in addition to your laptop and desktop computers. We've been so bombarded with the digital age that many of us have forgotten what life was like just 10, 15, 20 years ago before many of these technologies existed. When was the last time you put a quarter in a pay phone? I'm not one of those people who believes the machines are taking over or anything that extreme, I actually love technology, I've always been inquisitive with the way devices work. In fact, when I was younger there wasn't a device I couldn't dismantle. Now sometimes putting them back together became a challenge...maybe some of you have children at home fitting that description! Anyway you get my point.

There is a time to connect and a time to disconnect and it's our job to search for and create the balance between the two in our lives. Balance will allow us to gain more fulfillment from our work because it will prevent burnout. I've heard the concept of time management and I think it's a myth. We can't manage time, we must manage ourselves within the time allotted us. Time goes on with or without our input, whether or not we're feeling good or bad, having a good time or not.

A few friends of mine are experts in various areas of treating the body properly, let's hear from them now!

# Cherie Corso on Organic and Toxic-Free Living

I created Reiki charged organic products as a way to give women safe products to use. Along this journey which I initially began to create better nail products, I discovered a beauty product world ridden with harmful ingredients. My awareness of what I was putting on my body heightened as I realized how easily toxins are absorbed through the skin. While performing autopsies, as a result of many commonly used beauty products, medical professionals discover pounds of lipstick and plastics which, of course, the body is unable to naturally digest.

Every product we use gets absorbed through our largest organ, our skin, and effects the functioning of our bodies. I could not believe the weight I lost just by using my own organic moisturizer. My skin was now breathing and detoxifying. As a mother and a woman who loves fashion and beauty products, I was shocked to find hidden in the small print on bottles lots of harmful chemicals.

I have always believed in positive energy and what we put out is what we get back. All of G2 Organic products contain Reiki charged crystals which possess healing characteristics and promote positive energy.

One drop at a time you can be good to yourself and the environment and make a difference.

Cherie Corso, Founder
G2 Organics
http://www.G2Organics.com

# Marcus W. Wells on Health and Wellness

Let's face facts; we live in a very fast paced society that continues to get faster each year. We all like to think of ourselves as "movers & shakers", so we work more hours, take additional education classes, and push ourselves to produce greater results. However, during our attempt to conquer the world we often overlook the MOST important part of our lives; and that's our good health.

We are currently living in a nation where almost 70% of the population is overweight, and out of that, 30% are bordering on obesity. It's great to have goals and want to be an overachiever in life, but if you lose your health in the process it's all for nothing if you're DEAD. Without giving your personal health and wellness the attention it deserves you won't be around long enough to enjoy the fruits of your labor.

Incorporating health & fitness into your lifestyle is not as difficult as most people think. It does require some commitment, but it doesn't have to consume your life. There is a great book called the "Slight Edge" which talks about how little changes can make all the difference in the world over time. Start with thirty minutes of exercise three times a week, substitute flavored water for soda, and get a massage twice a month. Over time these small "Slight Edge" changes can totally transform your body and give you the quality of life you truly deserve.

To Your Good Health….
M.W Wells        aka    "The    Fitness    General"    Founder
Code Red Fitness
http://www.CodeRedFitness.com

I appreciate my friends spending some time with us today and I encourage you to incorporate their suggestions into your life as you create balance. As we close out this chapter, here are four balance-enabling action items:

## Action Items

1. **Laugh Hard and Often-** Laughter is just good for the soul. Have you ever had one of those deep down bust a gut, watery eyes type of laughs? I'm sure you have and once you regained composure, if you're anything like me, as you rubbed your stomach you said, "Wow! I needed that!"

2. **Unplug-** Turn off your cell-phone and computer, don't allow people unlimited access to your life.

3. **Set Hours of Operation-** At times in my life, I'm guilty of not effectively setting and keeping hours of operation. There is a time to work, a time to rest, and a time to play. Get them all in!

4. **Appreciate Your Apparatus-** Show your body you love it, get a massage regularly. Not only does it feel amazing, a massage has proven health benefits. Provide your body with the proper nutrition and follow a quality fitness regimen. Eliminate toxic products and people from your life!

# 7. Don't Just Believe, Know!

**"It's your thoughts behind the words you speak that create your attitude." –Jeffrey Gitomer, author of The New York Times best sellers *The Sales Bible* and *The Little Red Book of Selling.***

## Going From Believing to Knowing

If you really take some time to think over the course of your life, I'd be willing to bet that most of you have had life experiences which have caused you to transition from a place of believing to a place of knowing, of certainty. A personal story from my life:

May 17, 1997

Prior to this date I "believed" my life had purpose, I was 19 years young ending my sophomore year at Loyola College in Baltimore, MD. I had a summer job lined up selling jewelry at a kiosk in the Cherry Hill Mall although I was not scheduled to start for another 2 weeks. The plan was to come home, relax for a couple of weeks, and then jump into focusing on making money for the summer. My manager called that Saturday morning to say she was swamped and asked if I could start working immediately, of course I said I'm on my way. I head over in my dream car which I hadn't had for a full 6 months yet. Life's great, I'm feeling wonderful, clothes and car look good, I'm headed to make a few bucks, and it's a beautiful sunny day! I cross the Ben Franklin Bridge out of downtown Philadelphia into New Jersey. As I'm cruising down Admiral Wilson Blvd., a 6 lane highway connecting Camden with Cherry Hill, I'm in the inside lane closest to the wall approaching a dump truck riding in the center lane. All is well in my world and then BANG!...Darkness! Apparently the dump truck just made a drop and the  driver didn't realize his hydraulic boom was raised. The truck crossed under a pedestrian overpass a moment before I could pass it, the boom struck the bridge knocking it off of its base and sending a 90-ton mass down onto the highway, oh and of course onto my automobile with me behind the wheel. Of the 3 east bound lanes and 3 west bound lanes, mine was the only vehicle on which the bridge landed. Yes you're reading this correctly, a 90-ton pedestrian overpass landed on my moving vehicle! But wait, there's more miracle to this story. I'm guessing the combination of my vehicle's momentum and suspension system is the reason my car, crushed roof and all, continued to coast straight down the highway with me unconscious. To my left, the wall also known as the center divider and to my right, a guard rail beyond which lies a river. My car never touches either. As always and blatantly seen here, I was in God's hands. A gentleman from a nearby gas station comes out to my vehicle, which by this time slowed to a coast, reached in to turn off the ignition and call for help. I begin to regain consciousness to the sounds of the jaws of life cutting the roof from my car and an EMT telling me everything is going to be ok. He was also asking me if I remembered what happened and the only things I remembered were a truck, a bridge, a loud sound, and darkness. First, let me take this opportunity to publicly thank the gas station attendant, EMT's, and hospital staff (I wish I could mention you by name) for their role in my rescue. And secondly, I shared this story to tell of a personal experience in which I went from believing to knowing. As I mentioned earlier, prior to May 17th 1997 I "believed" my life had purpose. After being, as the doctor phrased it, probably the only guy in the world to have a bridge fall on him and live to tell about it, I KNOW my life has purpose!

My life's purpose is to directly and indirectly positively affect the lives of millions of people. Now maybe your experience wasn't or won't be as drastic, that's ok. It's still important to find and fulfill your purpose.

## Create Certainty

Which sounds more certain: I believe I can do it! Or I KNOW I can do it! I'm sure you'd agree that when you KNOW something, that's it, there is nothing else. If I ask you for your name, are you thinking, "I believe my name is...?" Of course not, the things in life of which you are absolutely certain you KNOW! When it comes to accomplishing dreams and aspirations the power of believing in your ability cannot be ignored and when you KNOW it's done you will move with such conviction that those around you will begin to KNOW it's done as well! Try this little exercise:

Think of something you desire or are working on, get in front of a mirror, and look yourself squarely in the eyes and say I believe I can do it. Basque in that feeling for a second and then shake your head and wipe your face as if hitting the reset button and then say I KNOW it's done, its mine, etc. Now recognize your empowered state. This is a simple action step which has worked for me on so many occasions. The energy you generate with that simple sentence lends so much power to your aspiration. When you know, you just know and if you don't act on that little seed of an idea, before you know it, it will have grown into an all-consuming oak tree of a gut sensation. This could be a thought, your love for a person, or an action you're supposed to take. Have you ever just had a thought or an idea that started small and all of a sudden it was all you thought about? You dreamt about it and you couldn't help but talk about it. This is what they call a clue, the universe is showing you your potential. Believe you can! KNOW you can! I hear all the excuses, I've used some of them myself...I don't have time....I don't have enough money....No one will pay for this....What if I fail...and on and on.

# The Five Outs

I'm reminded of a phenomenal training I once received on a conference call for Pre-Paid Legal Services, Inc. about the Five Outs by Marla Cam. Let's revisit them now:

1. **The Drop-Out**: Self-explanatory, this person definitely doesn't believe and they certainly don't KNOW they can accomplish their dreams. They join or start and they quit before the ink dries, any little challenge can knock them out of the game. These folks are settlers, they settle for mediocrity and a below par lifestyle. Drop-Outs convince themselves they don't need the luxuries in life. You'll hear them say things like money isn't everything. And yes I agree money isn't everything but as the saying goes, it ranks right up there with oxygen. Generally when they make that statement it's not coming from the standpoint that there are things in life more valuable than money. It's usually coming from that place which says, "if I can convince myself I don't need it then I won't miss it if I don't have it." Maybe you once were a drop-out. I'm here to tell you I KNOW you don't have to be a drop-out ever again!

2. **The Cop-Out**: He/She is always looking for an excuse not to do something. You'll hear things from them such as, "I can't go to the meeting or seminar because my favorite show or sports game comes on at that time." The cop-out is a masterful Blame-Game player, they blame everyone and everything except the one person truly responsible for their outcomes...the man or woman in the mirror! Here is a list of cop--outs, I would if only:

I had the money

I was athletic enough

I had good genes

My parents left me an inheritance

I grew up in a different neighborhood, during a different time

I didn't have kids

I knew how to use a computer

I was younger

I was more physically attractive

I started earlier

---

(Add a statement you've used or heard)

3. **The Fake-Out**: On the outside looking in it would appear that this person is doing everything in their power to succeed. They're reading the books and attending the seminars and trainings. They constantly talk the talk but are not walking the walk and as I've heard it said, your talk talks but your walk talks louder. Time exposes all and it won't be long before the fake-out can no longer hide behind the façade. People lie, numbers don't. As results begin to show, or in actuality lack thereof, the fake-out's cover is blown. This is why I've always liked sales, before long there is nowhere to hide. If you ask a fake-out a numbers driven question they start in with a story. I think it was Jim Rohn I heard say once before, "we kept the box for your answer very small so only a number could fit. Once you give us the number it will tell us the story." Every business has its numbers and it's up to you to learn and work the numbers because if you do, the numbers will work for you.

4. **The Hold-Out**: Of the previous three outs, I think the hold-out is the worst. This person, and everyone around them for that matter, knows of their unbelievable ability. For whatever reason the Hold-Out chooses to play small, they opt to play pee-wee

football rather than stepping up to the NFL. Some of these folks prefer to be a big fish in a little pond instead of working to become a whale in the ocean. The Hold-Out will never voluntarily take on the challenge of more responsibility at work, in the community, or organization. Have you ever been a hold-out in your life?

5. **The All-Out**: I'm sure you can figure out what this person is all about! The All-Out is the one who does not accept failure, they invest every fiber of their being into accomplishing the goal at hand. No simply means not right now to the All-Outs of the world. They don't just believe in their ability, they KNOW succeeding is already done, the process is a mere technicality. To say the All-Out has laser focus is an understatement, she will work hard AND play hard! He only knows to play the game to win. Period.

**Michael Jordan, All-Out**. One of my favorite commercials features Michael Jordan saying "I have missed more than 9000 shots in my career. I have lost almost 300 games. On 26 occasions I have been entrusted to take the game winning shot...and missed. I have failed over and over again in my life. And that is why I succeed." Some career stats: Six-time NBA champion (1991-93,

1996-98); MVP (1988, '91, '92, '96, '98); 10-time All-NBA First Team (1987-93, 1996-98); All-NBA Second Team (1985); Defensive Player of the Year (1988); Nine-time All-Defensive First Team (1988-93, 1996-98); Rookie of the Year (1985); 14-time All-Star; All-Star MVP (1988, '96, '98); One of the 50 Greatest Players in NBA History ('96); Olympic Gold Medalist (1984, '92). **Oprah Winfrey, All-Out**. She is an African-American actress, talk-show hostess, journalist, and one of the most successful entrepreneurs and television personalities in the world. She has been ranked as the most powerful celebrity by Forbes magazine as well as the ninth most powerful woman in the world. She is the first African-American woman to become a billionaire.

**Jay-Z , All-Out**. Jay-Z is a rapper and former president and CEO of Roc-A-Fella Records. He is regarded as one of the most prolific and successful American blend artists of the mid-90s and early 2000s and is known for his use of metaphors, free-styling abilities, word play, flow, and blending of street and popular hip hop. Apart from being former President and CEO of Def Jam Recordings, Jay-Z is also one of the owners and founders of the

Roc-A-Fella empire, which includes Roc-A-Fella Records, Roc-La-Familia, Roc-A-Fella Films and Rocawear. At heart, Jay-Z is an entrepreneur like his fellow hip-hop-moguls-turned-friends Russell Simmons and Sean "Diddy" Combs, who also have business holdings such as record companies and clothing lines. He redirected the hip hop culture from hooded sweatshirts and baggy jeans to button-ups and crisp jeans, and received GQ's International Man of the Year award. Source: last.fm

**Richard Branson, All-Out.** Branson is the self-made British billionaire who began Virgin Records and Virgin Atlantic Airways, among a host of other enterprises. He chairs the Virgin Group, which is the umbrella over Virgin Interactive, Virgin Megastores, Virgin Cola, and other divisions. Branson is also noted for the adventurous spirit he brings to both his work and his personal life. He has embarked on record-setting boat trips and hot air balloon escapades to boost publicity as well as for his own enjoyment. Due to his entrepreneurial spirit and enormous wealth, he is known as the "Bill Gates of Britain. Source: encyclopedia.jrank.org

**_____YOUR NAME, All-Out.**

**Your Stats**

_____

_____

_____

_____

_____

_____

_____

_____

If you're not excited with your life's stats don't let it discourage you, just take it as a sign of the magnitude to which you can grow. I know there is an All-Out in you and I'm here to give you the green light to release it! What Are YOU Waiting For?

# My Letter of Recognition and Demand to Life

There was a time in my life when I went from being an All-Out to some combination of the other Outs. I was sitting at a training for a part-time job I picked up at the time and the following is a note I wrote to Life:

*As we sit watching a training video, I can't help but imagine how or why people don't aspire to experience all that Life has to offer. I'm reminded of Jim Rohn saying, "some just don't." I can't get caught up majoring in minor things. I realize I've made many mistakes in life. I'm realizing I've taken my foot off the gas pedal and attempted to put my life on cruise. And I've learned that when you act casually, you become a casualty. Fortunately I've had the opportunity to experience this 1st hand and will never allow this again. So Life, I understand. I want it and know it's only going to take me getting after it with every fiber of my being! And the critical piece is to go after it with a tenacious 'I will until' mentality. I'm grateful and content and certainly not complacent. I got it Life, I'm on it! I want it…and you're going to give it to me!*

Take the time to write your note to life. In the last 24 hours, have you been an All-Out? The last week? Year? Whatever your answer, make the commitment to be an All-Out for the next 90 days. Yell it out, "I'm an All-Out!" Call someone and tell them!

Email Eugene@GiveYourselfTheGreenLight.com and share your commitment with our readers.

# 8. Create Momentum

**Chapter Quote "Success requires first expending ten units of effort to produce one unit of results. Your momentum will then produce ten units of results with each unit of effort." –Charles J. Givens**

## Make Some Heat

In his New York Times Best Selling *21 Irrefutable Laws of Leadership*, leadership expert John C. Maxwell refers to momentum as a leader's best friend. He goes on further to say this about the Law of the Big Mo:

*It takes a leader to create momentum. Followers catch it. And managers are able to continue it once it has begun. But creating it requires someone who can motivate others, not who needs to be motivated. Harry Truman once said, "If you can't stand the heat, get out of the kitchen." But for leaders, that statement should be changed to read, "If you can't make some heat, get out of the kitchen."*

## Call a Timeout

As of this writing, I'm entering my 5th year as a youth basketball coach. There are times during a game when I know we have momentum on our side and there are others when its working against us. If we have a series of turnovers or if the other team rattles off a bunch of points in a relatively short period of time, I call a time-out to regroup our team and hopefully break the momentum of the other team. Momentum works the same in life as it does in the sports arena, we just need to recognize which direction its headed and either add fuel to the fire if we have momentum or figure out a way to call time-out to regroup if it's working against us. You know what I'm referring to, there are those times in your life you feel you can do no wrong and everything is going your way. You're making the sales, getting the job offers, your business is firing on all cylinders, for the fellas maybe you're catching the eye of all the ladies at the party and vice versa for the ladies. You walk with a whole new attitude in your step. Taking a passive approach one might assume that momentum either happens or doesn't happen as a result of some external factor. I prefer the active approach, the route which places the responsibility for creating momentum squarely where it belongs...on my shoulders! I encourage you to take responsibility for creating momentum in your life. You may or may not be the leader of a team, a business, a church, a department, a family, etc. You ARE the leader of your own life. You can have momentum working in your favor every day, it doesn't have to be an every once in awhile occurrence.

## Create and Maintain a Momentum-Filled Experience

**a. Challenge Yourself/the Team:** It starts here. What do you want to create? What do you want out of life? Are you looking to start a business? Maybe you have an established business and are looking to take it to the next level. You may desire to get into better physical condition. The challenge may be 10 push-ups a day until you work your way up, using momentum from daily activity, to 50 push-ups a day. Take time to answer the questions: What do I/we want?_____ What's my/our challenge?_____ I don't expect you to have only one, there are multiple areas of your life/business where you may desire to create momentum. The challenge must be something which causes you to reach, don't fall in line with a lot of people who set goals they can achieve with their eyes closed. Where's the fun in that? A real challenge simultaneously excites and frightens us. Challenge yourself!

**b. Cast the Vision**: Your job is to paint the picture, provide the experience of what life will feel like once you get into full stride. Scripture says, "without vision, the people perish." In your personal life as well as your business life you must distinguish between eye sight and mind sight. Eye sight is what you see in the physical realm and mind sight is what you see before you *see* it. Vision lives in the realm of mind sight, you create, cast, and hold on to the vision you see in your mind. Sometimes you'll hear people say, I'll believe it when I see it, Les Brown says, you'll see it when you believe it. He's talking about creating the vision of that which you desire first and then you will manifest it into your physical reality. Take a moment to do this exercise, listen to an inspiring musical piece, preferably the instrumental version so the words don't interrupt your thoughts. While listening, close your eyes and just imagine what your life would look like tomorrow if you had all the necessary finances, the great relationships, an amazing spiritual connection with the source of your guidance, and any other characteristic of your ideal life.

**c. Keep it in Front of Yourself/the People:** Posting pictures or words that remind you of the goal is a great way to propel yourself to take the necessary action. Maybe it's a sales goal so you post a number. A new car or new home possibly so you have pictures on your closet, your bathroom mirror, inside your current automobile. Seeing these may motivate you to take more action.

**d. Focus Only on What You CAN Do:** It's so easy to get caught up in what we "can't" do or what we "don't" have. The key is to focus only on the things we CAN do! You should be asking yourself, "what can I do to propel myself and our team towards the vision?" "What am I good at right now?" Constantly ask, "What's the next step?" And then, just as important, take that step!

**e. Celebrate All Victories, Small and Large:** Rome wasn't built in a day. We must celebrate all victories leading up to accomplishing our goals. What constitutes a victory varies from person to person depending on the goal. Let's say your goal is to write a book. Do you wait until the book is on The New York Best Sellers List before congratulating yourself? Of course not! First simply celebrate the idea of writing the book and then celebrate accomplishing small goals along the way. Maybe you spend some time writing the concept, then the outline, then the chapter titles, and then you jump in chapter by chapter. Each mini-celebration feeds into your confidence which feeds into your desire to proceed which then gets you to the next milestone to celebrate and the cycle continues. Let's talk weight since this is a consistent topic on the minds of people all over. If the goal is to lose 50lbs, waiting until you're at 49 lost lbs to celebrate is counter- productive. Today you made wise food choices or you took the stairs instead of the elevator or you made it to the gym. Although this may be day 1 and you haven't lost an ounce let alone a pound, these are all reasons to celebrate and pat yourself on the back. The more you can make yourself feel good the more you'll be willing to walk the walk. You've read this book thus far... *Celebrate!*

# 9. Recruit an All-Star Team

**"We win and we lose together."**
**–Mike Krzyzewski aka Coach K, Duke University**
**Men's Basketball Head Coach**

## Even the Lone Ranger had Tonto

Lots of us suffer from the Lone Ranger syndrome, that is to say we believe we can do it alone. I used to say, "If it is to be, it's up to me." The proper mantra is, "if it is to be, it's up to we!" Sure the buck stops on the leader and yes it may be your job to create the environment of success but achieving massive success in whatever endeavor you choose is not something to attempt to go at alone. Think of all the great success stories you've ever heard, I'd be willing to bet that behind the individual was an all-star team. Look at your top CEO's, behind them are dynamite CFO's, CIO's, VP's and the like. Top sports coaches have an unbelievable staff and of course the actual team of players themselves. What would Michael Jordan have been without Scottie Pippen? Darnell Self without his Team NuVision Family? We all have strengths and challenges and having an all-star team allows us the freedom to contribute our strengths while simultaneously minimizing the effects of our challenges. Someone else will be strong in your challenge area and vice versa and as the acronym goes T. E. A. M. means Together Everyone Achieves More. I know that I'm a big thinker, visionary type of guy and I can paint the overall picture very well. Getting into the details of accounting is where I begin to step into my challenge area and although I need to focus on this area it makes sense for me to find a trustworthy person who has a passion for accounting. If we each work in our strength zone the majority of the time we can move much faster together. Looking at your life and business, what are your strengths? Challenges?

## Characteristics of an All-Star Team

1. **Belief in the Team**- Members of the Team must possess a deep inner belief in and knowing of the vision. Members must believe in the Team's ability to accomplish its mission. In the huddle, board meeting, community meeting, etc. all members of the team must be able to, with all integrity, look every other member in the eyes and say, "I believe in you!"

2. **Respect for the Team**- There are billions of people in the world and there are billions of personalities. Of course we

are not all expected to like each other. However in a Team environment each member must possess a sincere respect for one another. Egos and personal agendas must be left at the door.

3. **Pride in the Team**- Five of the most powerful words you could say to someone, "I am proud of you!" That phrase usually causes the recipient to straighten their spine and hold their head high. There are times when the team has seemingly exerted maximum effort and great team pride, pride which says, "We will not quit, we will not be denied, we are better than that!" is the only thing fueling the engine.

4. **Chemistry amongst the Team**- Chemistry occurs when all members are on the "bus" and, just as important, in the right seat. Chemistry requires an ability and a willingness to work together in addition to each member's strengths covering all vital aspects of a successful team. Talking basketball, Shaquille O'Neal is one of the greatest centers to have played the game. How successful would a team of 5 Shaqs perform? Probably not very. A basketball team with chemistry will have a point guard, shooting guard, small and power forwards, as well as a center and those 5 players work seamlessly together. Think of your relationships, at times you meet someone and the two of you just click. It almost feels as if you've known this person for years. That's chemistry.

5. **Community Oriented-** Said another way, team-focused. The old adage holds true, there is no I in TEAM. As the leader, at times, you must be able to recognize the importance of needing to slow down to speed up. You have to realize members of the team learn at various paces and a team, just a like a chain, is only as strong as its weakest link. When you start a family, it's no longer about you. All decisions must consider the needs of the family first. In my opinion, Family and Team are interchangeable words. In Michael Jordan's, I Can't Accept Not Trying, he had this to say regarding team, "There are plenty of teams in every sport that have great players and never win titles. Most of the time, those players aren't willing to sacrifice for the greater good of the team. The funny thing is, in the end, their unwillingness to sacrifice only makes individual goals more difficult to achieve. One thing I believe to the fullest is that if you think and achieve as a team, the individual accolades will take care of themselves. Talent wins games but teamwork and intelligence win championships."

## Ask Not What the Team Can Do...

Although we often don't recognize it, we live our lives on teams. Think for a moment about all the organizations or groups to which you belong. Your job or business, the subcommittees within your job or business. Your church and the various groups included there. Your neighborhood community group. Your relationship. Children? Of course they're on the team as well. And the list can go on. The magnitude of the role you play varies from team to team, sometimes you lead the team and others you are a role player, no less important however. What would a sports team be without the fans? Non-existent. What would a pastor be without a church congregation? Simply a man or woman having a conversation with self. I read a quote once, "A leader without followers is just a guy taking a walk." My suggestion is for you to take inventory of the teams you belong to and maximize your role within those organizations.

## Establish Your Master Mind

One very important team to create is your Master Mind Group. The best Master Mind Group explanation I've ever read can be found in one of Napoleon Hill's most widely read books, "Think and Grow Rich." Mr. Hill defines the Master Mind as "Coordination of knowledge and effort, in a spirit of harmony, between two or more people, for the attainment of a definite purpose." You've heard it, when two or three agree, nothing is impossible. Create your Master Mind Group and exponentially explode your potential!

# 10. Be Willing to Let Go

**"What if the hokey-pokey is really what it's all about?" –Bumper Sticker**

## Don't Block Your Blessing

I have a quote hanging on my wall by E. M. Forster which says, "We must be willing to let go of the life we have planned so as to have the life that is waiting for us." Sometimes we can get so determined, a certain rigidity sets in and we, in so many words, block our blessing. At this point we walk the fine line where determination becomes synonymous with stubbornness. I was asked once in a job interview to name a personal strength and challenge. Immediately I thought my level of determination can at times go from being a strength to a challenge. You may be like me, once you get a grasp on an idea, or maybe I should say the idea has a grasp on you, knowing when to push forward, change your approach, or simply let go is a challenge area all its own.

## Practice Humility

It is critical at this point to remain humble and seek guidance.

Humility is key because often it's our ego which gets us into trouble and our pride which keeps us there. We don't like to be proven wrong and the idea of abandoning something we've started makes us feel we made the wrong choice. I came to realize, in most cases, if we adjust our attitude there is nothing wrong with following one course and then deciding to change lanes or roads altogether. Shakespeare said it best, "nothing is either good or bad only thinking makes it so." At the very least we've learned all about the road we were on and are now in a better place to assist someone else navigating that same route in the future. Seeking guidance, also known as asking for help, tends to be a difficult act for lots of people. While on a drive through unfamiliar territory, women have accused men for as long as I can remember of being too prideful to stop and ask for directions. For some reason, men just choose to ride around lost. If the motivating factor is to go on an adventure or just see sites and roads you've never seen, ok, sounds good. But if one interprets stopping to ask for directions as a sign of weakness or looking foolish, they couldn't be further from the truth. Actually it takes strength to recognize and embrace our need for guidance.

## Only the Strong

I recognize that of the 11 Keys to Giving Yourself the Green Light in Life, Being Willing to Let Go can and often times is the most challenging to implement. Think about all the things in your life you do simply because that's how you've always done them. Is it the most effective and efficient way? Or what past events have you allowed to skew your future choices? I'm referring to anything which may have previously happened to you which provides the measure by which you gauge a decision. For example, let's say you had a bad experience in a network marketing opportunity so you disregard them all as ponzi schemes, or maybe you lost weight before but gained it all back plus more and you feel it will always happen to you so what's the point of trying, or you may have even ventured outside your comfort zone to communicate with someone and you were not received in a pleasing manner so you choose not to open up to others. We could continue with this list but I'm sure you get the point. You know your own stuff.

First and foremost, the key is recognition. As with any 12-Step Program, you must admit there is a challenge before having the

85

ability to progress past it. Embracing the challenge will give us the opportunity to uncover the feeling which has anchored our thought process. Once done, we can replace it with an empowering and uplifting feeling. Replace:

"I opened up to him/her 10 years ago and he/she rejected me and I didn't like that feeling so I'm never going to let anyone know how I truly feel."

with

"I love to feel good, it makes me feel good to let someone else know I care about them, the sooner I tell them, the sooner I will know their feelings, and the sooner I can decide if this relationship can progress! Whatever the outcome, I know he/she isn't trying to hurt me."

So now that we have recognized and replaced the disempowering feelings we can move to the 3rd piece of the letting go process and that is to replay the good thought feelings until they are anchored in our subconscious. In so doing, our decisions are coming from an empowered good feeling place.

I've taken the liberty to create two lists to help you recognize and replace items in your life which you may want to let go of and others upon which I encourage you to grab.

# The Let-Go List

- ➢ Debilitating Beliefs
  - o that don't serve you
  - o ie. I believe I'm not good at…and therefore I don't try or I'd love to…but I just can't seem to get it done
  - o He or she couldn't do it which means I probably won't be able to either
  - o (Insert Another)_____
- ➢ Subtractors
  - o people who you are allowing to drain you(this can be a difficult one because sometimes "close" family and friends may fall into this category)
  - o there is no middle ground, either someone is taking away from you or multiplying you
  - o a mentor of mine asked it perfectly, "Are they supporting your dream or choking your vision?"
- ➢ Disempowering Attitudes
  - o that's just the way I am
  - o the we've-always-done-it-this-way-so-it-must-be-right syndrome
  - o holding a grudge towards a person, place, or thing
- ➢ Negative Habits
  - o poor eating choices
  - o lack of a consistent exercise regimen
  - o smoking, excessive alcohol consumption, etc.
  - o (Insert Another)_____
- ➢ Clutter
  - o of your mind, allowing racing thoughts to prevent focus
  - o of your environment, have you ever had the feeling of just not knowing where to start because everything is so out of place?
  - o of your emotions, mixed feelings can hinder positive action

# The Grab-On List

- ➤ Energizing Beliefs
    - o I believe I am a great leader, public speaker, teacher, etc.
    - o I believe I can!
    - o I believe I will!
    - o (Insert Another)_____
- ➤ Multipliers
    - o People who pour fuel on the fire of your passion
    - o People who believe in you
    - o People who push you to excel
    - o (Insert Another)_____
- ➤ Empowering Attitudes Allow You To
    - o Cultivate a success consciousness
    - o Foster winning expectations
    - o Possess a learning posture
    - o (Insert Another)_____
- ➤ Positive Habits
    - o Quality eating choices
    - o Consistent exercise routine
    - o Daily personal development
    - o (Insert Another)_____
- ➤ Clarity
    - o Of your thoughts, know your desired outcome
    - o Of your environment, strive for a clean and neat apartment, house, car, desk, closets, drawers, wallet, purse, etc.
    - o Of your emotions, be honest to self about your feelings
    - o (Insert Another)_____

## A Clenched Fist v. An Open Hand

As we bring this chapter to a close, using the concept of a clenched fist v. an open hand provides the perfect imagery for letting go. When we think of a clenched fist it conjures something tightly held like many of the items on the Let-Go List. I think tension and stress, nothing gets in or out. A clenched fist is synonymous with a closed mind and of course we know that's one of the most expensive things we could possess. An open hand, on the other hand, pun intended, symbolizes peace and a willingness to receive. It puts you in the powerful position of being ready to catch all the benefits life is sending your way. A fist says, "I'm up in arms," whereas an open hand says, "Hello, nice to meet you."

We must remain willing to let go of that which doesn't serve and replace with that which does. If you are someone who has overcome any type of addiction, normalized your weight, implemented positive practices in your life, developed empowering attitudes, dropped the zeros to get around the heroes,

**Congratulations!** You have shown the **Willingness to Let Go!**

# 11. Sell, Sell, and Sell Some More!

**"When you were born, God said, "Yes!"**
**–Sarah Pound**

## A.S.K. Ask Seek Knock

You want to see grown men and women shiver?  Suggest they go into sales!  For whatever reason lots of people are afraid of sales although in some way, shape, or form most professions, as Slight Edge author Jeff Olson says, are either in sales or in support of sales.  Here we will talk about both traditional and nontraditional sales.  I've spent the majority of my adult working career in some form of sales from retail jewelry to business-to-business selling with T-Mobile, as I mentioned, to network marketing with Pre-Paid Legal Services, Inc.  I knew before I was given my first shot at a sales job that I would love it, the idea of packaging and presenting a needed and/or wanted product has always appealed to me.  My first sales job was working for Plumb Gold, a little kiosk in the Cherry Hill Mall in New Jersey back around 1997.  There is an interesting story with how I landed in that position but it turned out to be the one opportunity I needed to open many other doors.  I was a college student at the time, had been modeling part time, and knew I wanted to get into sales. Everywhere I applied kept giving the same response, "well you don't have any experience but we'll keep your application on file." And of course we know what that means…it will sit in some drawer in the back office somewhere or even worse land in the circular file cabinet also known as the trash can. I thought how can I get experience if no one will give me a shot. I was not discouraged however, and knew these no's were bringing me closer to my yes! Wink, wink, hint, hint. Actually I thought it was their loss not mine. So I'm working a part time modeling job in the Cherry Hill Mall for a few weekends and it just so happens I was situated near the previously mentioned kiosk. I began to strike up conversations with the employees on my down time, one of which, Pauline, was the manager. During one of our conversations, she asked if I'd ever thought about going into sales and I thought this woman must be reading my mind. I explained my challenges with various places I'd applied and she shared with me that she had never hired a guy to sell jewelry before and was ready to try something new. She went further to ask if I'd be interested. Wow! Of course I am interested! Pauline was amazed at my willingness especially because she knew I was a college student from Philly going to school in Baltimore, Maryland contemplating working in Cherry Hill, New Jersey on a more consistent basis. I was determined not to allow anything to stop me so I commuted on the weekends back home so I could work my new sales job. This proved to be a great move! Pauline was pleased, she said I was the best sales person, male or female, she had ever hired and I was pleased because now I could put not just sales but successful sales on my resume. From that point forward I was offered a sales position at most places I applied. I never got to publicly do this so I will take the opportunity to thank Pauline now: Thank You Pauline for taking a chance and giving me a shot! If I ever run into you again, I will be sure to give you an autographed copy of this book and a big hug!

The word sales, in the minds of many, is synonymous with rejection. For some, the word 'no' is worse than a punch in the gut. Quick side thought, for those who have done sales you'll know exactly what I'm talking about, you actually don't hear the infamous 'no' a lot. People will say everything but 'no'. Maybe, not right now, call me next week, next month, after the new year, when I get all my ducks lined up, let me talk to my wife, my husband, my spiritual advisor (and yes I've heard that one personally), my son or daughter, and the list goes on and on but people don't just say 'no' so in reality, there is much ado about nothing! Sales is simply a transference of belief. That's it. I believe something about an idea, product, or service and I'd like you to share my belief. Sometimes the transaction of transference of belief requires money to change hands, ie. I have a house, car, phone, or Identity Theft Shield service I believe in and I'd like you to believe in it and own it which will require you to buy access to it. Other times I may possess an idea into which I'd like you buy, ie. I'm a parent and I'd like you to buy into the idea of cleaning your room or I'm a teacher and I'd like you to buy into the idea of doing your homework. Although this often goes unnoticed, this is a sales transaction. Sure the parent or teacher may argue this isn't sales, the child has to do it because I said so. Well a sale was made there as well. As a basketball coach I have to sell the players on the importance of such characteristics as teamwork, honesty, and work ethic. I can judge from our results if I effectively made the sale.

# The Most Relentless Sales People

Children are relentless sales people until adults succeed in beating it out of them. What do I mean? Children are innately persistent, if they want it they will find 100 different ways to ask the same question and if that doesn't work they will just ask the same question over and over again. Although we can't always say yes, I encourage this persistence because I know this a necessary trait for success in anything in life. Sometimes adults just get 'no' happy and even when they can say yes they say no or never really take the time to explain why 'no' is the answer. Have you ever heard this conversation:

Child: Mommy or Daddy can I...?

Parent: No.

Child: Please?

Parent: No.

Child: Why not?

Parent: Because I said so, now don't ask me again.

As I said this, over time, beats the persistence out of some children. I'm certainly not saying that we need to say yes to everything a child requests, that could be hazardous to their health. I am however, suggesting that we explain some of those no's and that we find other ways to provide a yes.

Of course I don't think everyone should quit their jobs and go into some sort of traditional selling. As we discussed in the chapter Create an All-Star Team, you can't have 5 Shaquille O'Neals on a team. Likewise, everyone can't be a traditional sales person. Someone needs to hang signs on the expressway, build houses, repair automobiles, etc. I am saying that you should recognize the salesmanship aspect of whatever you do and hone your skill.

## Keys to Successful Selling

1. **No leads to Yes:** This No simply puts you closer to Yes

2. **Network/Build Relationships:** It's about who you know not what you know

3. **The universe practices checkerboard mgmt:** You make a move, your desired outcome moves closer to you

4. **Challenges show us our strength:** The universe challenges champs and chews up chumps, you are a champ

5. **You miss 100% of the shots you don't take:** Nothing beats a failure but a try, take your shot

6. **Don't take anything personally:** It's not really about you anyway

7. **Allow people to taste or feel:** Enables an easier "buying" decision

8. **Ask for the sale, rephrase, overcome objections, ask again:** It ain't over 'til you win

9. **The Fortune is in the Follow-Up:** Statistics show, on average, yes comes after 5-7 asks

10. **Practice child-like persistence:** "No" has no meaning to a child

# Conclusion

**There are only two things you "have to" do in life. You "have to" die and you "have to" live until you die. You make up all the rest.**
**-Marilyn Grey**

I often find myself thinking about all the unrealized dreams in the world, wondering what could ever be so powerful as to make a person give up on a dream. I'm not just talking about a wish or a hope or a fleeting desire for a fad, I'm talking about a deep down in the pit of your gut dream. That type of thing which has kept you awake at night. That thing which has you mentally plotting and scheming all throughout your day. The thought of not chasing this dream makes you queasy and nauseous. You know the kind of feeling I'm talking about? What makes a person give up on that? We've all known someone, maybe very personally, maybe the person we see in the mirror everyday, who has given up on a dream. Ask yourself this question...What would the world be like if those unrealized dreams materialized? If your book was written, who would it impact? If you run for President of the United States, how can you change the global atmosphere? If you manifested your business idea to end world hunger, provide a cure for cancer, obesity, etc.? Maybe your dreams aren't that grand, albeit no less important to you or the world. You may very well have a dream to mentor a young person, a teenage parent, an aspiring entrepreneur. Or even to learn a new skill such as playing an instrument or learning a new language.

Whatever your dream, I'm here to tell you, you CAN live it! I believe it is not only your God-given right but also your obligation to live your dream and walk in your purpose. You never know who might be watching you and deciding whether or not to go after their dream based on whether or not you aspire to yours. So many people today, as Henry David Thoreau says, are "slaves to their work and enslaved to those for whom they work." He continues, "the mass of men lead lives of quiet desperation." The staggering number of people who complain day in and day out about their jobs is amazing. We often hide behind, "the job isn't paying me enough." When, in actuality the discomfort stems from the realization that you're walking in someone else's purpose and attempting to live another person's dream. Your inner guidance system is sending the strongest signal it can, your gut feeling.

*Follow Your Gut, Create Your Vision, and Live YOUR Dream!!!*

## Life IS Giving You the Green Light!!

## Go!

# The Recap
# 11 Action Steps to Giving Yourself the Green Light in Life!

Keep a copy of these two pages nearby.

1. **Do It N.O.W.**
   - It's **N**ot **O**ver until you **W**in
   - Treat the present as a gift and cherish it
   - Conquer procrastination
2. **Talk About It and Be About It**
   - Speak your dreams into fruition
   - Take consistent action toward your goals
3. **Commit to Personal Development**
   - Spend more time working on self
   - Take the 21-day challenge
   - Aspire to unconscious competence
4. **Focus on Future**
   - Continue offering empowering information
   - Be the testimony
   - Use the past as a place of reference not residence
5. **Enlist a Tour Guide**
   - Learn by reading and listening
   - Learn by watching
   - Learn by doing
   - Learn by showing
6. **Balance Work and Rest**
   - Laugh Hard and Often
   - Unplug
   - Set Hours of Operation
   - Appreciate Your Apparatus

7. **Don't Just Believe, Know!**
   - Create certainty
   - Live life as an All-Out
8. **Create Momentum**
   - Challenge yourself and the team
   - Cast the vision
   - Keep the vision at the forefront
   - Focus only on what you CAN do
   - Celebrate all victories, small and large
9. **Create an All-Star Team**
   - Instill Belief, Respect, Pride, Chemistry, and a sense of Community
   - Get everyone on the bus and in the proper seat
10. **Be Willing to Let Go**
    - Don't block your blessings
    - Create and adhere to your Grab-On List
11. **Sell, Sell, and Sell Some More!**
    - Ask, Seek, Knock
    - Be relentless in your pursuits

# Recommended Reading

21 Irrefutable Laws of Leadership ~ John C. Maxwell

Think and Grow Rich ~ Napoleon Hill

The Power of Less ~ Leo Babauta

The Law of Attraction ~ Esther and Jerry Hicks

Slight Edge ~ Jeff Olson

Rich Dad, Poor Dad ~ Robert Kiyosaki

Clean ~ Alejandro Junger, M.D.

The Richest Man in Babylon ~ George S. Clason

As A Man Thinketh ~ James Allen

Screw It, Let's Do It ~ Richard Branson

The Greatest Salesman in the World ~ Og Mandino

The 4-Hour Work Week ~ Tim Ferriss

Awaken the Giant Within ~ Anthony Robbins

Blink ~ Malcolm Gladwell

You Can Only Hope to Contain Me ~ Chuck Herring

The E Myth Revisited ~ Michael E. Gerber

Coach ~ Art Williams

Leading with the Heart ~ Mike Krzyzewski

# About the Author

Eugene Bell Jr. is an entrepreneur who has lead successful sales and marketing organizations, trained and coached business professionals, and spoken to groups all throughout the United States. He has over 15 years of successful sales experience. Eugene co-hosts the Streets Are Talking, a well-known radio show in Philadelphia and posts regularly on www.GiveYourselfTheGreenLight.com. Affectionately known to many simply as Coach, Eugene is a big believer in givers gain and one of his greatest passions is investing his time coaching youth basketball.

Eugene Bell Jr. is available for speaking engagements and personal appearances. For more information contact:

Eugene Bell Jr.
P.O. Box 28762
Philadelphia PA 19151
1.888.741.0181

# *WHAT ARE YOU WAITING FOR?*

Made in the USA
Charleston, SC
29 October 2011